Animal QUaCKers

Dog-Eared Doggeral!

Dick Maltzman

Illustrations by Jean Ann Smith

ANIMAL QUACKERS
DOG-EARED DOGGERAL!

Cover art by Elena Lishanskaya courtesy of Thinkstock; internal illustrations by Jean Ann Smith

iUniverse books may be ordered through booksellers or by contacting:

iUniverse LLC
1663 Liberty Drive
Bloomington, IN 47403
www.iuniverse.com
1-800-Authors (1-800-288-4677)

ISBN: 978-1-4917-4120-7 (sc)
ISBN: 978-1-4917-4231-0 (hc)
ISBN: 978-1-4917-4119-1 (e)

Library of Congress Control Number: 2014913115

Printed in the United States of America.

iUniverse rev. date: 08/07/2014

CONTENTS

Dedication:...vi

The Wiggly Things That We Once Were 1

I Owe a Debt to T-Rex 17

Oh Where, Oh Where Has My Sabertooth Gone? 23

Quackers 27

Darian the Vegetarian 35

Epilogue 54

Don't Sell Your Shell 57

The Migration of the Ants 65

A Bunny's Tail...69

An Ode to Bow Ties..75

DEDICATION:

This book is dedicated to my grandchildren, Noa, Mica, Alexis, Jessica, Max and Zoe; my granddogs, Timber and Snowy Snowflake; my good friends, George the Bunny and Arnold the Squirrel; and the memory of Happy, Dickens, Napa, Tahoe and Moxie.

THE WIGGLY THINGS THAT WE ONCE WERE

(With apologies to Rick Santorum)

Once upon a very long time ago,
Before there were people like you and me know,
Before there were dogs, before there were cats,
Before there were things other things begat,

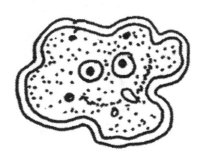

Before there were birds that fly where they please,
Before there was grass, before there were trees,
Before there were fish that swam in the sea,
Before there was anything recognizable to me.

There lived on this earth only one living thing,

A one-celled amoeba to life did cling,

As he reproduced with an idea quite daft,

He simply divided himself in half.

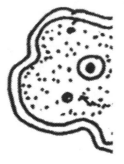 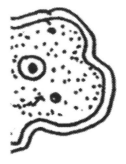

Now we can't do it, no animals can,
Nor can the fish, or birds, or a man,
See, all living things have many a cell,
And each has a mission and does it well.

Except, of course, that one cell guy,
Where his one little cell really must try,
To do all the things that many cells do,
In complicated animals – like me and like you.

Now in the beginning, the scientists say,
There were only amoebas with whom to play,
They lived in hot pools and had nothing to do,
But think of how they could be more like you.

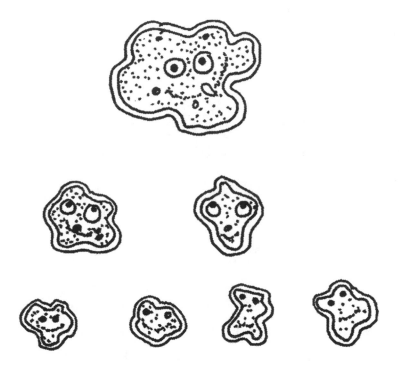

One day an amoeba, let's call him Fred,

Decided he wanted two cells instead,

And when he divided himself into two,

Said "Hold on a minute, I think I need you."

So now Fred had two cells instead of just one,

And discovered that two cells was twice as much fun,

So next when he divided, he kept all four,

Then divided again, and made four more.

Before you could count a hundred million years,
Fred kept on dividing, and so had his peers,
And Fred finally got what had long been his wish,
Fred was finally what we call – a fish.

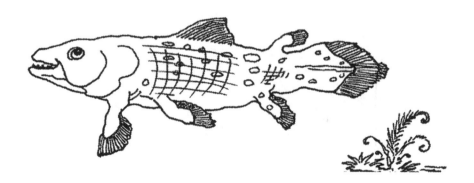

Now all of the Freds didn't divide just alike,

Some became salmon, some became pike,

Some kept on evolving and could eventually declare,

"Look at me guys, I can breath air!"

Other amoeba didn't take to that task,

They cared not for teeth or a face like a mask,

Instead they decided to come out like some moss,

Or grass, or a tree, or a salad to toss.

They became veggies from seeds in the ground,
They had no wish to move all around,
Staying in one place for them was quite neat,
You see in cell multiplying, Fred forgot to add feet.

The cells multiplied in some very strange ways,
Some things got quite big in the dinosaur days,
Some cells decided they needed some flair,
And that's how animals learned to grow hair.

As things began changing, a thought came to Fred,
"Wouldn't it be nice if we shared our bed?"
And so we developed two different sexes,
And which one came first really perplexes.

Now note that some animals live high in the trees,
And others crawl 'round on what might be their
   knees,
Some will dig holes and live underground,
Some will get fat and have tummies quite round.

Some of these aggregating cells we're about,
Grow very long noses that end with a snout,
And get very fat and yell that they can't,
Fit through the door, "I'm an elephant!"

Other living things are really quite small,
Or then there's the giraffe -- he's very tall,
Some living things live in their own shell,
Others live in colonies like ants like to dwell.

Spiders spin webs, bees live in hives,
Birds live very interesting lives,

But every living thing when it goes to bed,
Should give thanks to that little amoeba named Fred.

I Owe a Debt to T-Rex

Tyrannosaurus Rex gets a very bad rap,
Among the dinosaurs his mouth was a trap,
That killed off many a very mean thing,
Among those monsters, he was the king!

He ate hundreds of raptors, a very mean guy,
Who ate anything small that couldn't fly,
T-Rex tackled monsters forty-feet tall,
Whose gigantic feet squashed anyone small.

Now as it happened in the dinosaur days,
Our ancestors lived in far different ways,
Than you and I live, they had no home,
They had no cars if they wanted to roam.

Instead they had to travel by feet,
A conveyance which was not very fleet,
So they could be caught by raptors and such,
Who apparently liked their taste very much.

Or it could just be as they roamed about,

They'd be stepped on by something huge with a snout,

Or a girl would find something that despised her,

But still would make her a fine appetizer.

How any survived is difficult to tell,

To think how they lived is too hard to dwell,

On except for the fact that we wouldn't be here,

If those awful dinosaurs didn't disappear.

How is it they vanished but we're still alive?

I think that the answer you can derive,

If you remember that T-Rex killed from the top
   down,

And ate all the big guys while we're near the groun'.

Each time he killed one with monstrous feet,
That was four big squashers we didn't meet,
See T-Rex was really my kind of guy,
He was what they called a car-ni-vor-i.

He killed things that liked our ancestors' taste,
And each ancestor they ate was a terrible waste,
'Cause it could have been an ancestor of mine,
In which case I couldn't have written this rhyme.

So there you have it, I'm a fan of T-Rex,
But others are not, and there I'm perplexed,
It could be because he was misunderstood,
Or maybe it's because – my poetry's no good.

Oh Where, Oh Where Has My Sabertooth Gone?

The sabertooth tiger lived long ago,
And it really was big, as tigers go,
It ran very fast and was good at the hunt,
But never get near when he pulled that stunt.

The trouble, he found, was not with his size,
He was big enough to win any prize,
The trouble was not that he wasn't too bright,
The trouble, you see, was his bad overbite.

None of the other cats then around,

Were as big as he was or could make a sound,

As loud as his roar that was heard for a mile,

It's just that his teeth made it most hard to smile.

Now if you're a tiger you'd like to have dates,

With little girl tigers who could be your mates,

But the girls of his species when they saw his
    appearance,

Turned and made a quick disappearance.

The problem, of course, and we really mean this,
Was the fact that he needed a good den-tist,
But there were no dentists in those days long ago,
And we doubt that today there's a sabertooth you
  know.

In fact you'll find there's not a sabertooth left,
Of sabertooth tigers we're totally bereft,
Because it is clear, as we end this digression,
They died out for the lack of a dental profession.

Quackers

My wife and I we love to swim,
We find it keeps us pretty trim,
We swim a mile most every day,
Which is healthy, or so they say.

Behind our house we built a pool,
It's very long, which was our rule,
With room enough for both of us,
To swim our laps without a fuss.

Our house is located in California,
So I guess I needn't inform ya,
That our climate is mild and you have to go,
A very long way to ever find snow.

Well one day we woke in early Spring,
To a tremendous racket that did bring,
Me to the window overlooking our yard,
It was early morning, but sleeping was hard.

I wanted to see what could the noise mean,
But the sight was bazar, I thought it a dream,
What I saw below was an amazing sight,
Twenty-six ducks were about to alight.

Right on the deck of our beautiful pool,
Now ducks on the deck were not part of the rule,
So I threw on some shorts and grabbed a broom,
And quickly ran down out of the room.

I ran to the pool to shoo them away,
But shoo as I might, they just wanted to stay,
And one by one, quacking like they oughta,
Those twenty-six ducks jumped into the water.

Now that pool was mine, there for my laps,
Those ducks wore no suits or bathing caps,
They were stark naked, no bathingsuits at all,
And they outnumbered me, but I am quite tall.

Now our pool is kept warm by our solar panels,
But to my knowledge in all of the annals,
Of swimming pool owners who heat their own pool,
They're only for people, that is the rule.

So I decided to show each feathered friend,
Just how this story is supposed to end,
By jumping in the pool and starting my laps,
That, I thought, would get rid of these chaps.

But no, I was wrong, with one very loud quack,
All 26 ducks jumped right on my back,
And quacked and quacked as I swam back and forth,
They thought this better than flying north.

My swimming did not cause the ducks to flee,
Instead they appeared to take a liking to me,
They quacked all the louder as my laps I did ply,
And more and more ducks came out of the sky.

I finally crawled out from beneath that bevy,
Of ducks that by now was getting quite heavy,
And stared at my yard which had once been so cool,
It was loaded with ducks, and I felt like a fool.

I lost count eventually as ducks kept coming,
My wife and I started to take up running,
We also decided, and this was the rub,
To join the neighborhood swimming club.

'Cause the ducks loved our pool without any fish,
They go elsewhere to eat but return with a swish,
And they quack all the time except when its night,
So we still get some sleep, and that's all right.

We tried getting a dog, that did no good,
He played with the ducks, who understood,
That no one who lived in the house with the pool,
Would ever hurt them – that was the rule!

Darian the Vegetarian

On the rolling plains of the African veld,
The animals nearby one day beheld,
The amazing sight of Seymour the lion,
Oblivious to all of the animals pryin',
Prancing around looking quite proud,
And roaring his approval in a voice very loud.

Selma the lioness, one of his pride,
A very pretty lass that became his bride,
Had just delivered what brought out his roar,
A baby boy lion, the first in twenty-four,
For this pride had wives, they were precious pearls,
Who year after year delivered nothing but girls.

Now lions you know live in families called prides,
Which have many big males and lots of their brides,
The lionesses hunt and bring back all the food,
The males lie around with their manes that protrude,
They try and look fierce and have a very loud roar,
And its not good practice to make a male lion sore.

But Seymour, the lion, was as big as could be,
He was the biggest lion in the whole pride, you see,
And he looked at his cub and roared with delight,
"He looks just like me, and I'm sure he's quite bright,
And when he starts eating all you animals near –
My baby boy lion will fill you with fear!"

"What shall we name him," Selma did ask,
(Naming all sons was Seymour's big task,)
But the pride hadn't had any sons before,
So with that request he let out a roar,
"Call the reporter from the Jungle Clarion,
I'm naming my son after my father, Darian!

So there it was for the jungle-folk to hear,

There was now a new lion for everyone to fear,

He would grow up quite soon and be very strong,

And you never, no never, could tell him he's wrong,

For the lion you know, to all animals humble,

Is definitely known as the King of the Jungle.

Now a baby boy lion like any cat cub,

Plays and frolics and drinks milk for grub,

And Darian played with his sisters and cousins,

Who by the way counted to many dozens,

And they squeaked and purred and were really quite
  cute,

And they'd have little fights if they had a dispute.

Now little cub lions grow up pretty fast,

That cute little playfulness you knew wouldn't last,

And before very long their claws get quite pointed,

Their fangs sharpen too and soon they're anointed,

With what every young cub considers a treat,

They get to taste their very first meat.

Now all cats are hunters whether large or small,
They would rather eat meat than anything at all,
Candy to you might seem like the best,
Mom's apple pie you would think is quite blessed,
But a cat likes a mouse, he prefers that to eat,
And lions like big animals that walk on four feet.

In fact on the veld where the herd animals roam,
That is the place that the big cats call home,
For there they can find a stray wildebeest,
Or zebra or antelope on which they can feast,
The pride hunts together whenever there's a need,
And it was time thought Selma for Darian's first
    feed.

So she and the other young lion lasses,

Went out of the pride and into the grasses,

To sneak up upon a young innocent gazelle,

Who happened to be by and would taste really swell,

But the gazelle heard them coming and started
    to run,

And here's where the lionesses really had fun.

Gazelles are quite fast and can run very far,

But for a short distance the lioness is star,

She gets up to top speed as quick as a wink,

And can grab a gazelle and into her sink,

Her very sharp teeth and her terrible claws,

If the poor gazelle happens to pause.

And that is what happened on this bright sunny day,
The gazelle looked back and didn't get away,
The lions brought her down and now she was meat,
Which Selma and company took back for a treat,
For the big males who always took the first helping,
And then came the cubs who were standing there
    yelping.

This, of course, was the very first time,
That Darian had ever seen meat at its prime,
And nothing was more delicious they say,
Than a gazelle brought to dinner by lions this way,
And all the cubs roared and dove in for the treat,
Of eating their very first taste of fresh meat.

But something was wrong Seymour noted,
Darian sniffed dinner and immediately emoted,
"I don't like the taste of what you call gazelle,
It's hard and its fatty and I don't like its smell,
You tear off big pieces and it takes time to chew,
Why can't we eat grass like other animals do?"

With that the entire pride stopped in its tracks,
Such thoughts would certainly end lion attacks,
The thought of a lion changing its diet,
And start eating grass, why who would try it?
That ridiculous thought was against lion culture,
And wasn't appreciated by the hyena and vulture.

Well Seymour was shocked and Selma was crying,

The other cubs laughed because Darian was defying,

The law of the jungle, and we all know about that,

It says that the King of the Jungle's a cat,

And that cat's a lion and Seymour's the boss,

Darian should never make his daddy cross.

So Seymour was furious, and he roared very loud,
"Darian, you pipsqueak, you're not part of this crowd,
Unless you eat meat – it will make you quite strong,
To eat grass like herd animals would really be wrong,
So hear what I tell you," in his loud roar he cried,
"Get to like meat or get out of this pride!"

But like meat he couldn't, it agreed not with him,
And he tried every kind, this wasn't a whim,
He tasted of zebra, he spit out his first bite,
He tasted a wildebeest but it didn't taste right,
He tasted a dik-dik, a very small fellow,
One bite and poor Darian really turned yellow.

Antelope, too, was put on his plate,

But as luck would have it, it was just his fate,

To not like any of the herd animals at all,

He liked not the big ones and liked not the small,

And while all his family considered him crass,

The one thing he liked? He liked to eat grass.

So thus it happened that hunting was out,

His cousins shunned him, and Darian would pout,

He was ignored by the pride, laughed at by all,

"You're nothing but a pussy cat" one of them called,

There really was nothing to do but to sulk,

And eat lots of grass to build up his bulk.

Darian the lion happened to thrive,

On the grass he was eating to keep him alive,

And the berries and leaves that he found all around,

There was plenty of food right there on the ground,

And Darian grew to be big and tall,

But he had no friends, no friends at all!

One day young Darian happened to see,

Some very tasty leaves that were still on a tree,

So with a strong leap and his very sharp claws,

He climbed up that tree, and there he did pause,

'Cause from that high vantage and his landing place,

He was looking right into a tall giraffe's face.

"What are you doing up here?" the giraffe said.,
"A fall from up here and you could be dead,
You better climb down and I'd do it on the double,
If your mama sees you, you'll get in big trouble."
"They won't care, the pride hates me," replied Darian,
"It's because I happen -- to be a vegetarian!"

"Me too," said the giraffe, "and George is my name,
"And I eat leaves, and it would be a shame,
If you got up this far and didn't share my lunch,
The leaves of this tree have a very nice crunch,
And with your sharp teeth and your very strong jaws,
You could eat half the leaves without even a pause.

Darian didn't know it but this was a trend,

Of how he would go about making a friend,

He'd be eating some grass near a wildebeest,

And soon they would be sharing their feast,

And the wildebeest told others of his friend Darian,

Who to everyone's surprise was a vegetarian.

Gazelles soon joined in his friendly group

And next came zebras to join in the troop,

Then there were antelopes, they wanted in too,

And dik-diks and monkeys – it was a lot like a zoo,

With no fear of big cats, they'd all like to say,

As the sight of huge Darian would keep them away.

You couldn't keep this news secret for long,

To do so, of course, would be terribly wrong,

So the herd animals were quick to tell others around,

About the vegetarian lion they'd found

Who didn't eat meat – on this he wouldn't bend,

He was, to their knowledge, their first lion friend.

News quickly got out through the Jungle Clarion,
A reporter came out and interviewed Darian,
They took his picture and it appeared on page one,
But Darian's search was still hardly done,
For Darian who now was a very large male,
Needed a pride to finish this tale.

The article in the paper was what really worked,
A number of lionesses' interests perked,
For there were girl lions who hated to hunt,
And thought that killing was a terrible stunt,
They'd gladly eat grass for the rest of their life,
If Darian would take one of them as his wife.

And with lionesses came other males, too,
And soon his pride had a very large crew,
None of whom ever wanted to eat,
Any of the many herd animals they'd meet,
And Darian's pride was friends with all that dwelled,
Among the tall grasses of the African veld.

Epilogue

But what about Seymour and his mighty pride?
When news got out, there was no place to hide,
The other lions all laughed and made fun,
There really was no place for Seymour to run,
And recruiting new members did not go well,
The dad of a vegetarian was a very hard sell.

At first there were plenty of lions in his pack,
But they tended to leave when he turned his back,
And the hunting got slow, the herds all defied him,
And eventually there was only Selma beside him,
She still loved him and stuck it out to the end,
As it turned out she was Seymour's very best friend.

Seymour and Selma eventually retired,
There was a zoo in St. Paul and they both were hired,
And here's where the twist comes in this ballad,
It seems in St. Paul they took a liking to salad,
They'd eat salad for dinner, for breakfast and lunch,
On Sundays they'd even have salad for brunch.

The population of St. Paul did not find it distressing,
To see lions eating salad with croutons and dressing,
On occasion, of course, they'd be carnivore stricken,
And on those occasions they'd add some chicken.
But their new-found taste was not a disaster,
For they lived happily and healthily ever after.

Don't Sell Your Shell

Tommy the Turtle lives in a shell,
It really has served him pretty well,
But what poor little Tommy wouldn't give,
To have a bigger place in which to live.

You see Tommy has no kitchen or den,
To entertain friends on the occasion when,
Friends come over, and he has no fridge,
He has no game table on which to play bridge.

He has no guest room where friends could stay,
He has no family room for them to play,
He has no bathroom, so please don't ask,
Where he goes potty, that's his private task.

Of course his shell fits him quite well,
And that's where poor Tommy has to dwell,
Until, of course, he grows some more,
And then he must go to the new shell store.

There he will find a shell just the right size,
It will match his old shell, there's no need to disguise,
The fact is that Tommy is one very cool dude,
And to not wear a shell would be really quite rude.

You never see turtles swim in the buff,
They live in the ocean and it can be rough,
There shell protects them from big mean fish,
And little girl turtles think Tommy's a dish.

But Tommy wasn't happy, he wanted more room,
Larger shells didn't fit him, and that gave him gloom,
He wanted a house like you and me possess,
So what did he do? You never would guess!

He saw a big boat parked right next to him,
The owners jumped off to take a big swim,
So Tommy decided he had nothing to fear,
And the devil within gave him an idea.

He climbed up a rope tied to the anchor,
And made it aboard and there he did hanker,
To search the big boat, was living there better,
Than living in water where it was much wetter?

So Tommy climbed around, it was not easy,
He didn't have feet, so he was a bit queazy,
But he slivered and slided around his big prize,
And what he saw really opened his eyes.

There were very large couches on which to sit,
But turtles on couches didn't quite fit,
There was a stove to cook what you eat,
But cooking to a turtle was hardly a treat.

The beds looked comfy and were made with a flair,
But Tommy the Turtle wasn't comfortable there,
And except for a picture that was painted on a dish,
Look as he might, he saw no other fish.

So large as the boat was, and it cost lots of money,
Living in that style to a Tommy seemed funny,
He got lonely quite quickly and longed for the sea,
So he quickly jumped off and cried, "Hooray, I'm
    free."

"I don't need a big house, I love living small,
I'll stick to my shell, it's the best house of all,
It goes where I go and keeps me quite well,
And lets face it folks, it looks really swell!"

So Tommy the Turtle still loves to swim,
And when you go snorkeling you might see him,
Moving in his shell with tremendous grace,
And always, yes always, with a smile on his face.

He cares not for a big house, he'll keep it small,
He needs not a kitchen, no, not at all,
He needs not a guest room, who needs a guest,
Alone in your own shell just must be the best!

The Migration of the Ants

Sitting in my hot tub I saw an amazing sight,
It seems I did some splashing and it wasn't very right.
I splashed a bunch of water and it was very hot,
Upon a little anthill right near my hot tub spot.

At first I saw one little ant who stuck his head
    right out,
I splashed him with another shot, "What's that all
    about?"
The little ant must have thought as he raced back in
    his hill,
And a second later out he came with many more ants
    still.

They came out in one long straight line and it was
  quite a sight,
Those ants may be little but I think they're pretty
  bright!
Because each ant upon his back a very large load
  carried,
They carried out their babies, so I guess they must
  be married.

They next had loads of food and such that they had
    stored before,
It seems the ants left nothing there, they couldn't
    carry more,
They headed straight across the yard, I watched
    them as they went,
They were headed for a crack quite small right there
    in our cement.

Into that crack they disappeared, in the hundreds I
    could see,
How did they know that crack was there? It was a
    mystery to me!
But there they went and disappeared, down that
    small indent,
But there was one thing clear to me, to return was
    their intent!

And return they did throughout the year, those ants
    were all about,
I tried every strategy, but it was just a route,
If I attacked, they marched away and found another
    spot,
Could I rid my yard of ants? Let's face it, I could not!

I thought of trying something more, maybe a
    pesticide,
But when I saw those ants again, I vetoed homicide!
Instead I let them roam around, moving at their will,
And trust me we have ants about, for they are with
    us still!

A BUNNY'S TAIL

Bunnies and rabbits are different you know,
'Though both of them hop along as they go,
They both have long ears that flop in the air,
But rabbits don't have that bunny flair.

Bunnies, you see, are very clever,
They live underground to escape the weather,
They wear little fur coats that never grow old,
And that way, of course, they're never cold.

Young little bunnies also go to school,
That's why the bunny is nobody's fool,
There they learn how to hop and to read,
Two things of course that they really need.

Now you may not know it, few really do,

But the tail of the bunny is something quite new,

It was invented and not that long ago,

By a bunny named George who I happen to know.

Now at bunny school just before lunch,

Bunnies do jumping, and jump quite a bunch,

Of times up and down to get their legs strong,

But if they don't jump right, they land quite wrong.

If they land wrong they hit hard on their rear,
Where no tail was present as it did appear,
For as I mentioned, whether female or male,
In those days the bunnies had no tail.

On one of those occasions George the Bunny,
Had an idea the others thought funny,
"What," he exclaimed to his young bunny friends,
"If we all glued cotton to our little rear ends?"

"Then if we jumped and happened to fall,
"We'd land instead on our cotton ball."
Now all of the bunnies laughed as their friend,
Pasted a cotton ball on his little rear end.

But then when he jumped and took a fall,

He never yelled "ouch" or cried out at all,

And soon the other bunnies to home would jump,

And insist that their mommies cotton-up their rump.

So that is why if you see bunnies today,

They always wear cotton tails when out to play,

And that bunny named George is famous indeed,

For solving for bunnies a very great need.

Today you will never see bunnies outside,

Without their cotton tails, it's really their pride,

But you'll never see a cotton tail on a rabbit,

Wearing cotton tails is not part of their habit.

An Ode to Bow Ties

The author loves his bow ties,
He wears them all the time,
To go outside in a four-in-hand,
He really thinks a crime.

He wears them when he's working?
He wears them when at play,
He wears them in every color,
And ties them the right way,

He wears them when he's jogging,
He wears them at the gym,
He even has waterproof ones
To wear to take a swim.

Doe he wear them with his pjs?
I hear the skeptic crow,
Well I'm sad I have to say
Only his wife will know.

He has in life just one regret,
He shouldn't be a man,
When choosing his type of animal,
There was a better plan.

He choose to be a human,
He must have been a dunce,
He could have been a tall giraffe,
And wear many bow ties at once!